Building Data-Driven Organizations

Daniel W. Rasmus
Pedro Martins
Hugo Cartaxeiro

Copyright @ 2021 Singularity Digital Enterprise.

All rights reserved. This book or any portion thereof may not be reproduced or used in any manner whatsoever without the express written permission of the publisher except for the use of brief quotations in a book review.

Illustrations by Eduardo Dâmaso and
© Rashmi Singh (cover), © Mikhail Mikhnevich, © David Sandonato, 7552290a,
© Drawlab19, © Veekicl, © Frescomovie | Dreamstime.com

First printing, 2021.

Publisher
Singularity Digital Enterprise
Alameda dos Oceanos, nº27 - Escritório 3
Parque das Nações
1990-197 Lisboa
Portugal

www.singularityde.com

Dep. Legal n' 493035/21   ISBN 978171603044

Preface

In 2016, and after several years working at Microsoft, we decided to create a Data Consulting and Artificial Intelligence company. Singularity Digital Enterprise is the result of our entrepreneurial spirit and willingness to challenge the market. Today, Singularity DE is a reference in the market.

Our mission is to help organizations transform internal and external data into tangible business assets to gain and sustain a competitive advantage in today's market. We do this with products and services to develop and support innovative data analytics solutions, extracting real business value from data through complex algorithms and AI, and presenting it with beautiful visualizations.

This book reflects five years of learnings derived from contacting our customers, partners, team members, and aims to be an actionable guide to Build a Data-Driven Organization to help managers on this journey.

With total dedication to the consulting, visualization, and advanced data analytics solutions, we brought this book to life, enriched with input from Daniel Rasmus to provide a unique broad experience.

It is our contribution to the digital transformation initiatives across organizations. Learning insights such as "Collecting data is not enough" and "Meet your data where it is and don't wait for your data lake," are good examples for supporting managers into action and building a strategy to create a data-driven organization.

Finally, our product, Power Management Cockpit ® was built over the years and has been nicknamed *The Eye of the Business*. It accumulates business knowledge and actual use cases experience to help managers avoid data traps, read dozens of reports, and spend hours gathering information and discussing the internal process, not the results.

The Power Management Cockpit ® allows managers to focus on the essential – run the business and decide on undisputed facts easily accessible on a single source of the truth – the Power Management Cockpit ®.

Thank you to all who shared this road with us over the last five memorable years: our customers, partners, and team. Let's make the following years even more impressive.

Count on us!

Pedro Martins
Hugo Cartaxeiro

A universe of data

We live in a universe of data. DNA defines the very structure of living beings; it encodes information and programs genes to generate the splendor of a rose, a beloved pet, or the color of the eyes of the person you fall in love with. Four nucleotides, adenine (A), thymine (T), guanine (G), and cytosine (C), make up the 3 billion base pairs that comprise human DNA. Several scientists sequenced the human genome in 2001, just 20 years ago. We continue to gain new knowledge by exploring our genetics as data. For instance, current analysis reveals that only about 1% of DNA causes genetic diseases. The data analysis of the human genome highlighted the essential disease-causing elements and created a focus for researchers.

Viruses also cause disease as their DNA interacts with ours. Data formed the basis of the innovative vaccines from Pfizer and Moderna that fuel the recovery from the severe acute respiratory syndrome coronavirus 2, or SARS-CoV-2, which causes COVID-19. The virus, like all coronaviruses, is named for the crown-like spike proteins that project from their surface. In *Structure, Function, and Evolution* of Coronavirus Spike Proteins[1], Fang Li writes that "During virus entry, [the receptorbinding subunit] S1 binds to a receptor on the host cell surface for viral attachment, and S2 [stalk] fuses the host and viral membranes, allowing viral genomes to enter host cells." Computer viruses derive their name from natural viruses because they invade existing code and insert new code into a system.

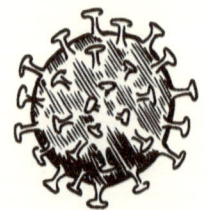

---

[1] https://www.ncbi.nlm.nih.gov/pmc/articles/PMC5457962/

The innovative COVID-19 vaccines leverage Messenger RNA (mRNA) as the mechanism for protecting people from infection. mRNA provides the genetic material that specifies how to make proteins. An immunization introduces new code that programs cells to imitate the virus spike so that the body can build up resistance. The immune system stores a memory of how to fight COVID-19 without ever having encountered it.

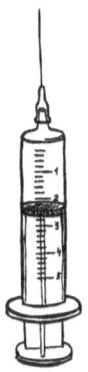

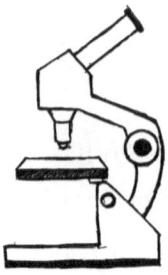

Seeing viruses and their interfaces with humanity isn't new. Historically, the exploration of nature at higher magnification levels drives science, and science often drives business. Viruses like SARS-CoV-2 were not known when Louis Pasteur and Edward Jenner developed the first vaccines. It was not until 1892 when Dmitri Ivanovsky, filtering out disease from a tobacco plant, first discovered the difference between disease vectors and the tissue that houses them. The modern understanding of viruses did not arrive until 1931 with the invention of the electron microscope which allowed the first views of a virus.

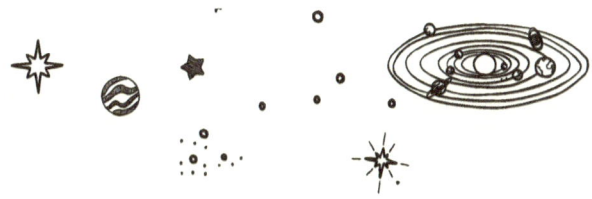

At roughly the same time that virus discovery gained momentum, physicists and astronomers invented new instruments to help explore the structure of the universe and the particles that comprise matter.
In 1929, scientists realized that other galaxies existed outside the Milky Way when Edwin Hubble measured the distance from the earth to what was then known as spiral nebulae. Scientists now routinely report new galaxies, as well as planets orbiting distant stars.

At the smallest scales, where the macro and micro converge, a tool like CERN's Large Hadron Collider (LHC) accelerator monitors particle decay in search of answers about the foundation of the universe. In July 2012, CERN's ATLAS and CMS experiments reported the discovery of the Higgs boson, a particle that imparts mass on other particles.

We learn more because we collect more data. The additional data allows us to answer some questions and prompts new ones. Questions inspire hypotheses. Only data can inform the inferences that confirm or reject a hypothesis. Without data, there is no learning.

Businesses now capture data more transparently — and they see processes at ever more granular levels. The wealth of data increasingly raises questions that challenge intuition. Gut feelings about why something works or doesn't no longer suffice. A business cannot ignore its data. Data supports testing hypotheses, applying scientific tests to understand how a company may work more effectively. Data also leads to innovative insights about how goods and services perform in the market and how they deliver value to customers.

For all the data that exists, however, organizations continue to struggle to harness it. The generation of data by integrated cloud services and the Internet of Things requires a reexamination of assumptions about how businesses manage themselves. The next revolution in business will not be AI-driven automation but data-driven insight that drives continuous improvement, learning, and adaptation.

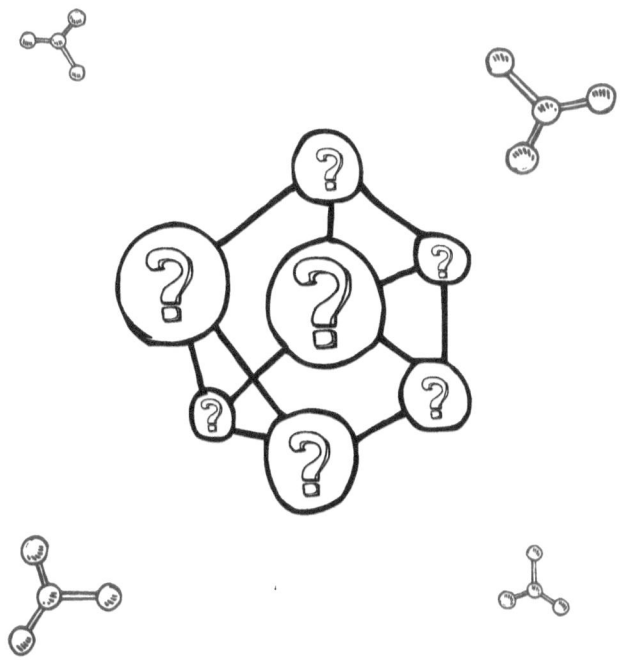

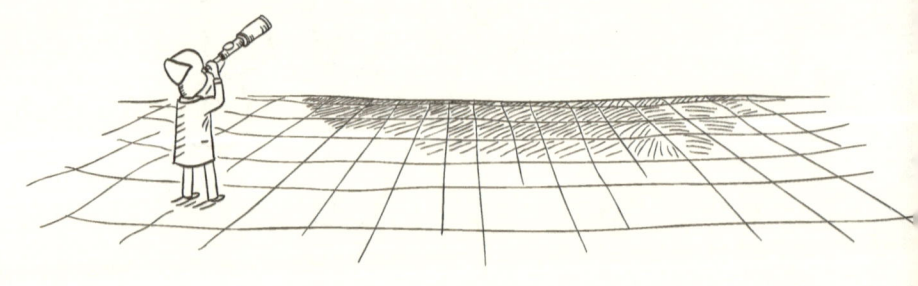

The state of data-driven organizations

Medicine needed data to learn how to fight disease. As instruments improved, physicians learned more about how to diagnose illness. Early MRI scanners captured 2,000 images of a human head, and that was considered a breakthrough. They now routinely capture over 20,000 images and often include 3-dimensional information. Better resolution. Better data. Better diagnosis. Better treatment.

Businesses are also improving how they encode data and make it more discoverable. Paper notes, tables, artifacts stored in file folders, bins of inventory cards, and printed work orders gave way to digital content stored in databases. Legacy databases strewn across hundreds of incompatible systems converge in Data Lakes, and processes consolidate in software as service (SaaS) applications.

According to Cisco, businesses create five quintillion bytes of data every day. IDC forecasts 175 zettabytes of data will exist by 2025[2], up from 33 zettabytes in 2018.

In May 2017, The Economist wrote that data would become the "fuel of the future...giving rise to a new economy."

---

[2] https://www.seagate.com/files/www-content/our-story/trends/files/idc-seagate-dataage-whitepaper.pdf

In the Harvard Business Review (HBR) article, *What's Your Data Strategy?* [3], Thomas Davenport points out, however, that "less than 1% of its unstructured data is analyzed or used at all.

More than 70% of employees have access to data they

```
less than 1% of its unstructured data is analyzed or used at all
                                                              <1%
|            Unstructured data                                   |
```

should not, and 80% of analyst' time is spent simply discovering and preparing data."

If that is true, businesses need to do more than engage in digital transformation—they need to become much more focused on data architectures and access to data in more useable ways. Early results looking at data-driven organizational outcomes suggest a disconnect between aspirations to become data-driven and the ability to execute on adopting a data-driven approach to business. In their 2021 survey, The Journey to Becoming Data-Driven: A Progress Report on the State of Corporate Data Initiatives[4], NewVantage Venture Partners found that only 24% of respondents reported creating a data-driven organization. At the top of their analysis, at 48.5%, sits data-driven innovation. No initiative reported a success rate of 50% or higher.

---

[3] https://hbr.org/2017/05/whats-your-data-strategy - [4] https://www.newvantage.com/thoughtleadership

The NewVantage Survey also reported that "92% attribute the 'principal challenge to becoming data-driven' to people, business processes, and culture. Only 8% identified technology limitations as the barrier."

Principal challenges to become data-driven

- 8% technology limitations
- 92% people, business processes, and culture

High-level, conceptual transformations in the NewVantage Survey do not get to the heart of data-driven results. MIT Technology Review Insights reports - In unpredictable times a data strategy is key - involving 357 business leaders and decision makers from all industries, and digs deeper into these grounds. MIT found 4/10 of survey respondents have indicated in 2021 that they need to look at more sources of data, particularly including demographic, geospatial and competitor information. Similarly, 37% of leaders are evaluating machine learning and analytic models, and 34% need help on the vast sums of data they gather and process.

Results of the data lessons learned by companies

Interestingly, the COVID pandemic served as a test to all corporations on whether they were prepared to handle uncertainty, change, and have more sophisticated data approaches. According to the MIT Technology report, more than one-third of respondents reported they significantly lack in processes for collecting, accessing, and using data, and are falling behind with their data strategy.

DATA LESSONS LEARNED	%
We need to look at more data sources	42%
We're evaluating machine learning and analytics	37%
We need help acting on data	34%
We need to redefine our data goals	27%
We need better tools and infrastructure	26%
Our data governance is lacking	19%
We don't have the right in-house skills	15%
Our data is siloed	11%

Source: MIT Technology Review Insights "In unpredictable times a data strategy is key", July 2021

For most circumstances, corporations are stuck in strategic gaps, strategy planning and implementation, or simply do not have a data strategy.

VALUE EXPECTED FROM DATA

Smarter Decision/making	79%
A better understanding of customers	61%
Better products and services	42%
More efficient operations	33%
Reduced costs	29%
New business	26%

Source: MIT Technology Review Insights "In unpredictable times a data strategy is key", July 2021

Those who have a successful data journey are experiencing developments such as smarter decision-making, a better understanding of customers, products and services, and reduced costs.

Adopting a data-driven perspective requires more fine-grained business goals and objectives. Aggregated key performance indicators (KPIs) with little transparency or detail need to expand. Organizations execute in the detail, and fortunately, it is in day-to-day interactions and transactions where most data lives.

If organizations want to better manage through data and achieve business results, they need to reframe their mental models for how a business works, which management levers really matter, and how they approach problem-solving. They need a new mental model for business.

Reimagining the business as data-driven: building a new mental model

Every organization that wants to become data-driven must assert the value of data and accept its role in business transformation. Business transformation includes technical and business components.

IT practitioners offer advice on the practical considerations for data, such as storage, retrieval, representation, and visualization—but becoming data-driven also requires profound mental model changes, strategy reappraisal, and exploring how to empower workers with the data they need to manage their work. It is not enough to believe in data; organizations must invest in data management, collaborative analysis models, ease of access—and most importantly—adopt models that demonstrate and actualize how data informs decisions.

Leadership by example is essential. Boards, executives, leadership teams, and division managers need to back strategy with questions, questions with hypotheses, hypotheses with experiments, and experiments with data.

Leaders need to create transparent processes that share what they know and how they know it, as well as what they need to know and their learning plan.

Becoming data-driven reinforces the desire to build a customer-centric organization. Much of the most vital data originates with customers, like insights about what people want, their opinions and relationships with products and services, and with whom they share their experiences.

To achieve the strategic attributes more effectively, the organization must also adopt a complementary set of data-driven principles.

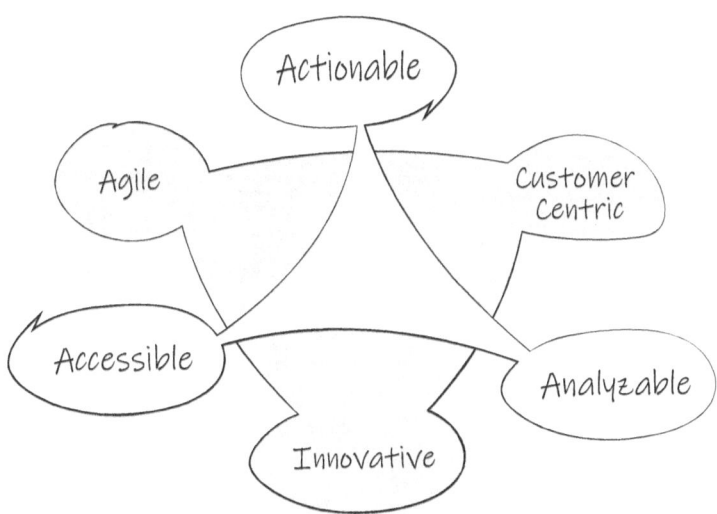

Becoming data-driven by design

In Dan Rasmus' book, *Management by Design*, emphasizes balance in design. Many of the failures of business transformations derive from an over-emphasis of one idea or activity over another. Industries saw this with quality management, knowledge management, and security management.
Those ideas proved vital, but they were not so imperative that they replaced other concepts. While most organizations eventually find a way to balance existing processes and practices with new ideas, they can achieve balance more effectively through proactive experience design.

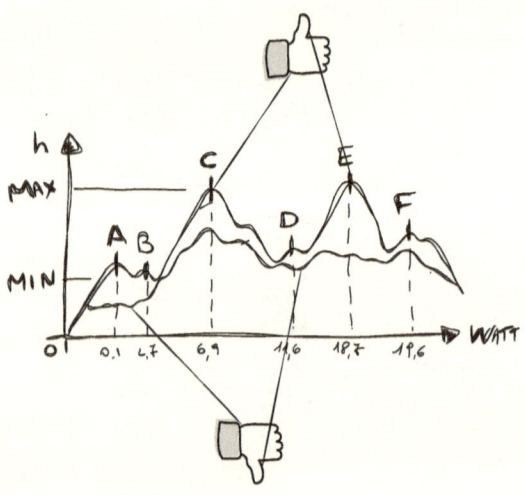

The new data-driven experiences will likely challenge assumptions codified in processes and practices. Aggregate reporting supported by anecdotal drilldowns, for instance, might evolve into data-driven experiences that allow managers, leaders, and process owners to explore operations transparently at a granular level. Clear business outcomes drive design, with processes, practice, and technology leveraged as design elements to reach those outcomes.

Design thinking can also help avoid the trap of overanalyzing the wealth of available data. By understanding the outcome first, be it revenue, loyalty, or reducing cost, the organization can focus on identifying the best data to inform decisions. The purpose and result of experience design acts as a relevancy filter in selecting data for operational excellence and learning.

Learning derives from data that offers feedback on operational performance. Design thinking embraces the totality of experience, not just how it functions in each instance, but how it relates to other systems and experiences.

Data should inform decisions about process and practice improvement. Learning also arrives from strategic shifts, from changes in business models, volatile business climates, or changes in customer profiles. Changes in KPI values likely indicate an emergent factor influencing performance, a factor that may require adaptation or innovation. When that happens, organizations should review the related experience designs to determine what the change means.

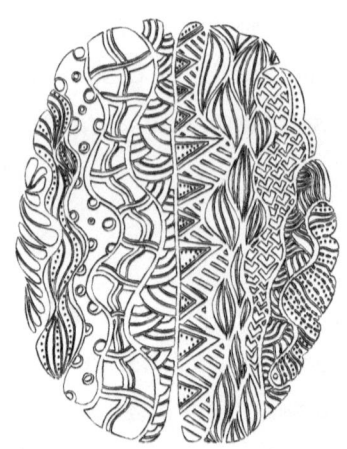

In some cases, changes in data value may reflect an underestimate for performance that gets embraced; in others, it may indicate an emergent negative response to a design element that compels a rapid response. The underlying data, and causes of the change, need to be understood regardless if it is positive or negative.

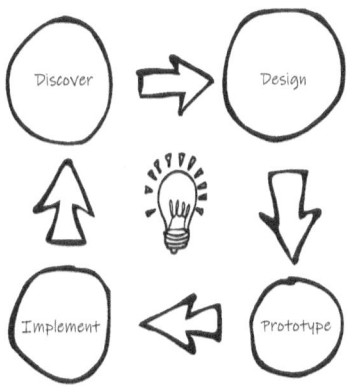

Design thinking proves critically important when novel data reveals that familiarity may not meet the moment's needs. Breaking down an emergent insight into its process, practice, and technology components, and then applying design principles like balance, emphasis, and proportion, reshape experiences to leverage new opportunities or mitigate a developing risk.

A roadmap to become data-driven

Design should shape data-driven experiences.
As illustrated below, a high-level roadmap toward becoming data-driven. It offers a lens to elevate the fundamental steps each organization must undertake during its journey to becoming data-driven.

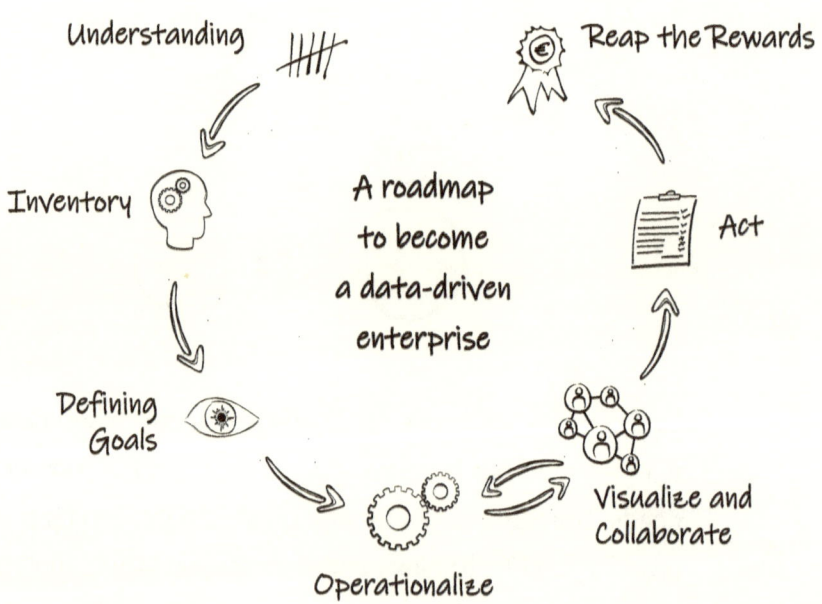

Each step along the way offers the opportunity to create new experiences that build on the previous step. Although the journey to becoming data-driven never ends, the conclusion of the first pass of data-driven design efforts will likely result in fundamentally different experiences, and perhaps a new relationship between employees and the work they do.

Policy and practice design reflect evolving mental models by capturing intent, offering guidance, and enumerating the implications of non-compliance.

Understanding and inventory.

Design begins with understanding and understanding begins with an inventory. Organizations need to start by understanding what data exists, where it is, and what it means. This process should be incremental. Consider using functions to drive the inventory. Organizations should not wait for a complete inventory before taking the following steps within functions or other organizational units.

Defining goals.

Defining goals should begin in parallel with the inventory. The inventory will inform the goals by tying data to specific indicators. The inventory may also suggest additional goals that emerge due to a better understanding of what can be measured.

Operationalize.

Operationalizing data puts it in the hands of those who can act on it. In this step, collecting relevant data and its analysis becomes part of routine work. Model use becomes common — and as models deploy, they help answer questions and inform the assumptions underlying forecasts.

Visualize and collaborate.

Data-driven organizations remove silos along with the temptation to hoard data for power. A more integrated view of data also requires a greater degree of collaboration.

Individual functions, or entire units, may discover data that explicitly link their ability to perform—and it may challenge assumptions that suggest more open organizational design. Shared insights about obstacles should also encourage collaborative problem solving and the sharing of lessons learned.

Act.

People act on the data, making changes in experiences and outcomes. Engaging with insights and feedback results in actively changing how the organization works.

Reap the rewards.

Reaping the rewards is a transitory step in a world of continuous improvement, but it is important to celebrate victories as they occur. Milestones and objectives will also bring opportunities for tangible increases in revenue, customer loyalty, employee engagement and satisfaction, and other indicators that reflect the ability to measure outcomes, learn from them, and improve them.

At each level of the roadmap, and for each decision, designers need to consider the following:

- **The objectives for the function or process.** What does good look like? Document as the foundation for testing against models and results.

- **The hypothesis to test.** Model to see if sample data explains the underlying factors related to the objectives. This phase helps decision systems mitigate risk from poor models, incomplete or inaccurate data, or from emergent variables. The hypothesis process aids in testing the value of a model before operationalizing it. See this HBR tutorial[5] for additional insight on hypothesis testing in business.

- **Which data reflects the state of the function or process.** Once the model works, determine which data is available, and from where, to support operationalizing the insight.

---

[5] Harvard Business School Online. A Beginner's Guide to Hypothesis Testing in Business, Tim Stobierski. https://online.hbs.edu/blog/post/hypothesis-testing

- **How to rationalize the data.** Integrate data from different sources, and if necessary, rationalize the representation and design the data stores to make access and visualization easy.

- **How to operationalize data collection, integration, and access.** Create automation to keep data sets up-to-date and available to stakeholders.

- **Analyze the operational data.** Analyze the data to determine the health of a function or process at the time of observation.

- **Make a decision.** Making decisions is the most difficult to document as myriad decisions at different levels of abstraction rest on data. Each function, each discipline, and each business has its own choices to make. Regardless of the decision, data-driven organizations know what data they need. They use data to make decisions—the quality of decisions, however, remains up to the decision-makers, the fitness of their models, and their willingness to listen to what the data is telling them.

Critical decisions, like which product innovation will likely drive customer retention, which supply chains are underperforming on deliveries for an audit, or which power plants to select for modernization, first require very different data, but they all flow through the seven steps above. In some cases, pieces of the answer may already be available in dashboards or reports from one system or many different systems. Still, the current state of data access likely underperforms on actual need. The use of data in most businesses requires too many manual interventions, too many meetings to reconcile data, resulting in too many suboptimal decisions based on incomplete or inaccurate data.

These steps seek to simplify the use of data—design crafts experiences that result in less manual work and fewer bad choices.

Data provides one other critical element to design. It permits organizations to tie the execution of work to strategy. Through data, people building products, maintaining facilities, trading commodities, or selling in a retail storefront, can see how their work contributes to the organization's goals. Technology does not currently support the spontaneous revelation of data architecture intent. Revealing how data relates to work requires a design that purposefully aligns work with strategy, creating a more meaningful context that connects work with organizational value.

Data-driven change management

It is clear becoming data-driven changes an organization. How organizations manage change will differentiate successful data-driven initiatives. Any time change management leverages the principles of the change itself, the more likely the change will stick. The success of quality management, knowledge management, and customer relationship management often stems from those disciplines applying their practices to managing change. When applied to the implementation of those ideas, the principles they encompassed acted as reinforcements and accelerators. Becoming data-driven is a whole organization effort, and it should be data-driven as well.

Like those from Waggl and CultureIQ, new tools seek to capture data about an organization, including how well change initiatives are perceived, accepted, and adopted. And like any data-driven process, they start with a model and measure against benchmarks and targets. These tools, and others like internal sentiment analysis and psychometric testing, provide data that helps organizations understand how employees and contractors react to change, which processes work, and the relevant KPIs. Data helps reveal how to manage change better.

Managing change should also include examining external perceptions, especially when it comes to investors and customers. Customer loyalty analysis requires data and models that reflect customer perceptions. Does a new perk, for instance, propel loyalty? If so, how long does the uptick last? Did a price reduction mimic the expected outcome of a loyalty program? How are price and loyalty related?

Social media can help organizations understand how their customers, partners, suppliers, and investors perceive the decisions they make, as can quantitative studies and qualitative work such as focus groups. Like all data within the business, external data needs to be rationalized and made available for access by all who need it.

Data-driven change management should help identify where to make program adjustments, inform hypotheses that anticipate the outcomes of decisions, and guide adaptation feedback on just how well the organization is managing its way forward.

Embracing uncertainty

There is no data from the future. Every bit and byte is historical. All forecasts make assumptions about the world that drive extrapolation. As we learned during the COVID-19 pandemic, assumptions can be laid bare. Paper mills could not meet the demand for personal products. Consumption of personal protective equipment (PPE) surged, as did global demand for USB video cameras. Food scarcity impacted many regions. Chip manufacturing shifted, precipitating global shortages in many sectors. And in the middle of the crisis, civil rights and social justice protests reshaped the global dialog about race.

Data continued to flow, but it was not the anticipated data—it no longer matched the models. Consider gasoline consumption, which is one of the most historically recorded data series. It has been reported weekly since 1991.
As Agricultural Economic Insights points out, gasoline consumption offers a valuable proxy for "economic and social activity." During the pandemic, the data showed an enormous dip in gasoline consumption. Yesterday was most definitely not like today.

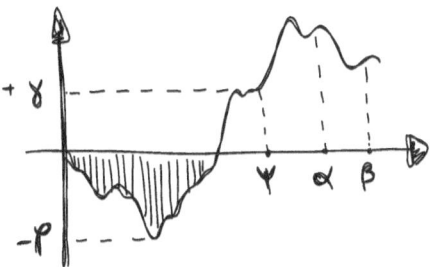

The first choice for managing under uncertainty is to accept it. Become skeptical of assertions and assumptions that register more than minor probability errors.
The COVID-19 pandemic might be called a Black Swan in the forecasting world: some anticipated but infrequent and equally unlikely event that gets written off as meaningless in

day-to-day business. Earthquakes and wildfires fall into that category as well. But in much of the world, we now see enormous impacts of wildfires, some manifest as zombie fires in Alaska, burning underground during the winter and flaring up again in spring. Those fires contribute to, and result from, climate change, and they may well need to be put into climate data models sooner than not.

But because there is no data from the future, datadriven solutions don't work for forecasts for twenty or ten or even five years. Long-range forecasts also suffer from the complexity and interplay between factors. New technologies arrive that change social dynamics. Underlying inequalities in social systems erupt to change expectations about work, life, and the economy.

Economic factors shift—which country has the most influence? What are people buying? What do investors want to invest in? How are environmental factors, like the availability of rare earth elements, the control of the coastal regions, and water rights, impacting businesses? What regulatory and governance factors drive business decisions, and how will the political functions of business influence legislation? Social media businesses are now facing the potential for considerable shifts in regulatory oversight that may change their businesses entirely.

The acronym "STEEP" stands for Social. Technological. Economic. Environmental. Political. It often represents these uncertainty factors.

STEEP is used as the basis for scenario planning, a strategic planning practice that helps organizations imagine their futures and anticipate the conditions of strategic decisions under uncertainty. Scenario planning crafts multiple deep narratives about the future that offer a variety of contexts that help decisions and imagine their outcomes against different futures. An investment product that might do well in one future, might fail in others. Can the designers of that investment product think of ways to make it more universal? Is this a contingent product that only gets rolled out if some future similar to the successful one comes about? Or does the firm redesign the product to be more resilient against different futures?

An investment product that might do well in one future, might fail in others. Can the designers of that investment product think of ways to make it more universal? Is this a contingent product that only gets rolled out if some future similar to the successful one comes about? Or does the firm redesign the product to be more resilient against different futures?

Organizations that adopt scenario planning often bring a humbleness to decision making because they know the future will challenge each decision they make—they know their decisions will never be right under all circumstances. No matter what decision they take, some factors will change, forcing them to reevaluate assumptions once again, and likely, make a different decision. Making mistakes in future decisions is not failure but learning.

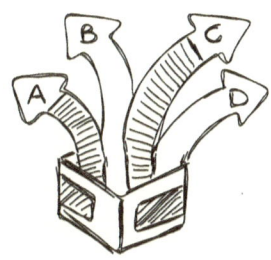

Since there will never be any data from the future, scenarios offer the best way to explore it. And because they assert positions, they can also be considered data-driven in that the monitoring of data for indicators of STEEP directionality comes from the unfolding of insights. That process helps anticipate the future because those indicators will point to actions that an organization has likely already tested and practiced for during the scenario work, making them better prepared than their competitors for its eventuality.

Scenario planning offers decision-makers a way to test long-term decisions against a variety of possible contexts. As climate change and social justice begin to influence the decisions made by investors, those who used scenarios to anticipate the rise of environmental, social, and governance reporting, known as ESG, are better positioned to meet the demands of investors and regulators.

Enter ESG

There is little new about ESG as an idea. The environmental, social, and governance factors that reflect an organization's adherence to internal and external ethical and environmental standards evolved from ideas like balanced scorecards and intellectual capital accounting.

The regulatory environment, however, changed recently with the adoption of Sustainable Finance Disclosure Regulation (SFDR) by the EU. Other regulatory bodies, most notably the U.S. Security Exchange Commission (SEC), have also increased their interest in ESG. In parallel, mounting evidence suggests that organizations that focus on ESG factors are more successful than their competitors who do not.

There is a correlation between the emphasis on ESG and the rise of data-driven organizations. Without data at very granular levels, organizations cannot capture and analyze their impact on the environment effectively, nor can they model their place in society. And it is the increasing amount of data that prompts demand from consumers and investors for businesses to reveal their performance in areas that impact the health and safety of individuals, the viability of communities, the continuation of nature, or the sustainability of the business itself.

ENVIRONMENTAL
Conservation of the natural world

Climate change and carbon emissions
Air and water pollution
Biodiversity
Energy efficiency
Toxic emissions and waste management
Water scarcity
Climate change vulnerability

SOCIAL
Considerations of people and relationships

Customer satisfaction
Data protection and privacy
Gender and diversity
Employee engagement
Community relations
Human rights
Labor standards
Health and safety

GOVERNANCE
Standards for running a company

Board composition
Audit Comittee structures
Bribery and corruption
Executive compensation
Lobbying
Political contributions
Whistleblower systems

In the past, ESG reporting was often a best effort, even in highly regulated industries. The advent of data-driven organizations sets a higher expectation for accuracy and transparency in reporting.

Reassessing technology's role in data-driven initiatives

While the NewVantage Partners study reported 92% of business leaders believe the resistance to becoming data-driven hinges on culture, process, and people issues, technology likely plays a more significant role in the story.

Aging legacy systems require sophisticated extraction routines to bring data into more open repositories. Data often gets represented in different forms, which requires transformation ahead of integrated analysis and collaborative insights. And in many cases, workarounds still exist, which create data beyond the reach of existing systems.

A good example is the Power Management Cockpit created by Singularity Digital Enterprise which aims to give to any manager the X-ray of the company's most important management indicators in a centralized view and informed business decisions supported by trustable, meaningful and relevant business indicators. The question of how to represent the data, how and where visualizations manifest, and on what platforms persists. As technology evolves, even core systems become obsolete. Iterative versions of systems and architectures, drive re-evaluation and replacements. Underlying data systems converge, and the applications

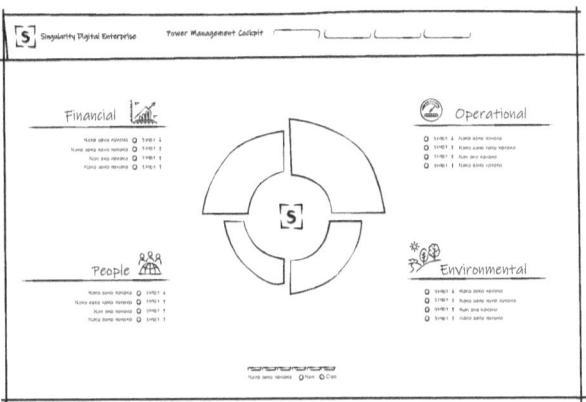

that store, process, and recall data increasingly integrate—as data relationships grow more explicit, governance becomes more critical. Like the first scientists to discover a cell's inner workings, a concept once considered simple became orders of magnitude more complicated when examined up close.

Self-reporting the low impact of technology impediments to becoming data-driven may reflect wishful thinking and a false sense of control over technology migrations. To paraphrase a cliche, becoming data-driven isn't a destination, it is a journey. All journeys face multiple obstacles; most cannot be anticipated at the time one departs. Technology will continue to evolve, and it will play a significant role in the continuing journey toward becoming data-driven.

Listening to the future

Looking at organizations and operations through the lens of science offers a fresh perspective, but the relationship between data and success is nothing new. The best organizations, be they governments, nonprofits, or commercial enterprises, always leveraged data for competitive advantage. Sometimes the data was collected and used for short-term turnaround projects or new product launches. Spy networks operate on the principle of knowing more than the adversary, though data often arrives cryptic and incomplete.

What differs in the future is the amount of data and how much of that data will be relevant. Data will flow through systems and accumulate in databases waiting for organizations to leverage it. That half of enterprise data that remained untouched in 2018 may mean much of the new data will also fail to add value in the future.

But that need not be the case. Organizations that choose to become data-driven can start their journey today. Start by selecting critical parts of the business that would benefit most from improved decision-making and better forecasting. They can design new decision processes based on the currently available data. As more useful data becomes available, processes will evolve. Organizations need to meet their data where it is. In some cases, that may require extraction and transformation, reviewing permissions, or deploying new systems to capture supplemental data.

All our pasts were once futures. For most people focused on improving a business, a government agency, or an NGO, the value of good data to inform decisions returns time and again as a critical factor in success or failure. This is not data about the future but data about the moment. What do customers really think? How much inventory actually sits in supplier warehouses? How much will it likely cost to build that new facility?

Data is not enough. Data must combine with analysis focused on the correct data to inform decisions. A small number of factors may offer the essential insights that lead to better management. Finding those factors, understanding their implications, using them to facilitate collaboration, and ultimately to make better decisions—that is the hard work that every aspiring data-driven organization must undertake.

The Challenge

We live in a data universe. Organizations have shifted their attention towards becoming more capable and efficient when handling data to create new business opportunities and obtain better results.

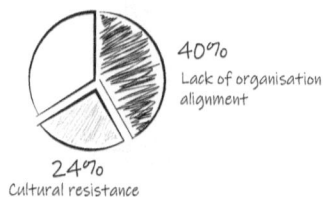

Challenges to become data-driven

40% Lack of organisation alignment

24% Cultural resistance

Supported by a Harvard study[6], 40% of executives recognise a lack of alignment between corporate objectives and culture, meaning there is a clear growing awareness in becoming goal-oriented and data-driven. The same study also conveys that the most significant factor contributing to companies having considerable difficulty becoming data-driven, 24% was indicated by executives, is that organizations are confronted by cultural resistance. In this case, organizations should start to focus on becoming data-driven and identify barriers preventing them from becoming one.

[6] https://hbr.org/2019/02/companies-are-failing-in-their-efforts-to-become-data-driven https://online.hbs.edu/blog/post/hypothesis-testing

It is essential to improve business processes within enterprises, and it should then incentivise new business information models that promote higher decision-making and problem-solving abilities.

With the data tsunami we are facing today, on a day-to-day manager work level, this is even a more challenging and critical situation.

It continues to be challenging and complicated to have the correct information at the right time at a manager's fingertips to support business decisions.

In a typical workday, managers need to read dozens of different reports, and spend enormous time gathering and organising information. Their teams invest a lot of effort to produce aggregated reports quickly and effectively to keep up with the speed of business.

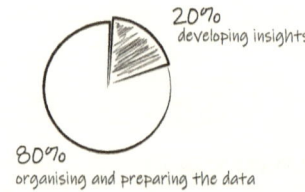

Data Scientists Time Spent

20% developing insights

80% organising and preparing the data

According to IBM[7], data scientists spend 20% of their time developing insights. Seen that most of all global data is unstructured (around 80%), most of the time is spent just on organising and preparing the data. Thus, organizations need to focus on spending more time gathering and concluding insights from the data.

Since decisions have become more complex than they were two years ago (Gartner, 2021)[8], organizations should prioritise spending most of their time not structuring data but getting insights. Especially when most of these organizations do not

[7] https://www.ibm.com/cloud/blog/ibm-data-catalog-data-scientists-productivity
[8] https://www.gartner.com/smarterwithgartner/how-to-make-better-business-decisions

have the adequate capabilities and knowledge to structure and prepare data, it simply costs a lot of time. Given that 80% of data is unstructured, organizations that do not possess efficient data skills will choose incorrect data, and it will not be closely aligned with the company's main objectives.

Most of the information and data is unstructured, so companies that have not developed a roadmap and focus on adopting data-driven values will consume a lot of time organising, identifying, analysing, and concluding the information. Not only that, but the company will have ended up choosing the data that was least valuable. It becomes a frustrating race against time that consumes considerable resources. Most critical business decisions are based on outdated information that quickly loses its relevance.

This is one of the biggest problems that companies have when communicating with customers. Developing advertisements and marketing campaigns based on 40% of inaccurate data will make companies lose millions, and customers end up leaving. Most of the time, erroneous data is regarded as outdated. For marketing campaigns, it is crucial to have the most recent data aligned to current trends, tastes, and behaviours portrayed by customers.

Besides, that is very common to have different values presented for the same indicator, revealing untrustworthy information and incorrect Data Governance.

60%
of executives report bad decisions are about as frequent as good ones

A Harvard Business School[9] (2020) survey concluded that 60% of executives report bad decisions are about as frequent as good ones. Added by Exasol[10] (2020), their research further states 58% of companies make decisions based on outdated data.

58%
of companies make decisions based on outdated data

[9] https://online.hbs.edu/blog/post/team-decision-making
[10] https://www.exasol.com/news-exasol-research-finds-organizations-make-decisions-based-on-outdated-data/

The difficulties that companies are experiencing need to be carefully measured, as a wrong approach could worsen the situation. These companies need professionals and experts on the concepts and values that data brings.

The potential of data is continuously raising questions that challenge the organizational capabilities of intuition. Enterprises can capture data more transparently and see their processes at a more granular level.

Nowadays, decisions need to be data-focused, bring us facts, and not limit our decision with intuition, instinct, or common sense. Data also guides us with a more sophisticated understanding of the performances of goods and services in the market and how they generate more value for clients.

The Solution

One of the most challenging processes is simplifying complexity. Human beings are complex, and we are different from natural, biological, or technical systems. We are not like birds or termites or computers.

So we are keen on transforming simple things into complex processes; it´s the way our brains are used to exercise. The human brain is the most complex system in the known universe. It is a highly connected structure. So the capability of resuming, simplifying is vital, and to management, this is a powerful skill.

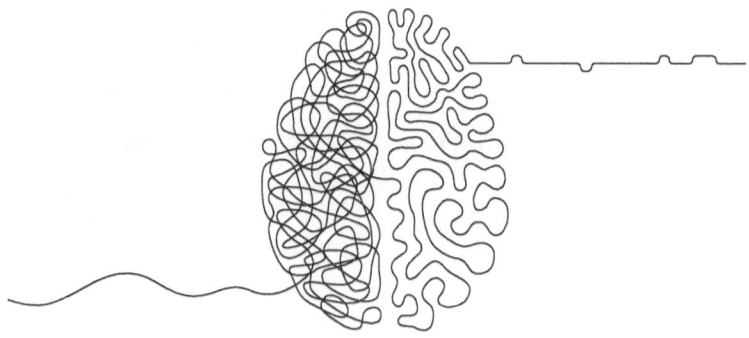

With this challenge in mind, we start with a teaser:
In just 30 seconds, have the most critical information or Key Performance Indicators of a company in a unique place or dimension.

Take it back to the basics; we started thinking like a company X-ray to see the most relevant and meaningful KPI of a group of companies, company or departments, as an actual X-ray sees beyond the ordinary sense.

After that, we developed a human-centric approach to a complex optical system—THE EYE as a specialized sense organ capable of receiving visual images, which are then carried to the brain.

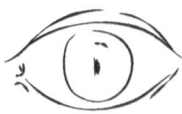

The same principle applies to companies; we build a unique solution that can make it possible to monitor the business performance in a rich, intuitive and uniform manner like an Eye—The Eye of the business. Within just 30 seconds, Management can have a glance of their business. We visualize the solution with the principle of simplifying information with a vibrant visualization.

The "Eye" in the centre of the Cockpit can be organized from four to eight quadrants of different business units or groups that are the main focus of the business to control.

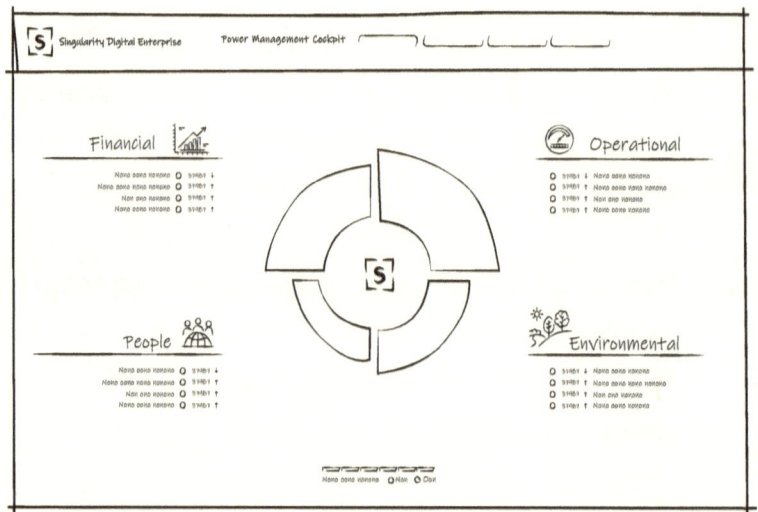

For each KPI, we can define a concrete target, and the line provides a target that is defined for each business unit. When it is outside of the target line, we are above the target, and if it's inside the target, it gives us the opposite trend as we are below the mark.

We can also have an individual status per KPI, with deep-dive information about each main KPI evolution in the last periods plus more knowledge, without leaving this Eye of the business vision.

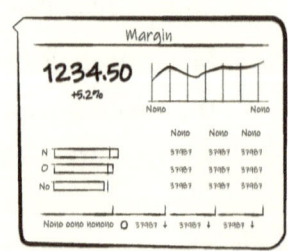

https://www.singularityde.com/solutions/power-management-cockpit/

Last but not least, from this initial visualization, it is possible to explore and deepen each of the business areas and indicators that influence the overall performance of the whole company.

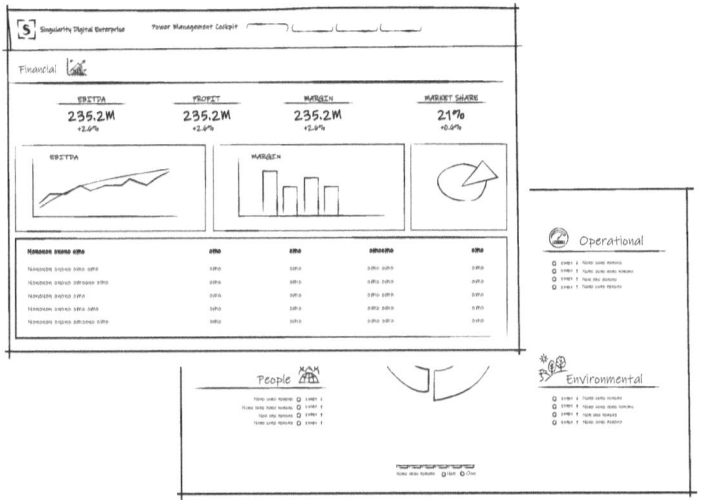

With this solution already proven in different sectors and departments in organizations, the top managers could now go above and beyond, like an X-ray, to make data meaningful to support business strategies as natural as receiving a unique visual image of their business like an Eye.

Benefits

The impact of the Power Management Cockpit for Managing Companies are significant. Businesses have already realized the importance of having alignment across the organization, and with alignment comes increases in revenue, employee engagement, and a host of other benefits.

The aggregated business information in an intuitive and interactive cockpit allows monitoring all the company performance facilitating the decision-making process on time. In fact, in just 30 seconds, it will enable the top management to perceive the business performance status in specific business analysis.

Any Manager could take an immediate view of the organization and improve business performance through this intuitive and interactive solution with the proper insights to support the decision-making process.

At the same time, they can also explore the respective indicators to understand deviations and detailed evolution of the business under analysis.

Due to the COVID-19 lock-down, top managers learned to work anywhere anytime and lead their companies from any location. But most of the organizations were not ready for this challenge.

With this new reality, managers need a tool like Power Management Cockpit to monitor their business, creating and aligning goals that feed into organizational strategy and increase ROI.

On the other side, due to changes in the business environment, organizations need to adapt quickly and enable performance.

Some companies in the most diverse sectors and departments are already reaping the rewards of having the Power Management Cockpit solution implemented.

With this reporting solution is possible to monitor all business performance in a rich, intuitive and uniform manner; it's the "The Eye of your business."

Authors

Daniel W. Rasmus

Thought Leadership Advisor at Singularity Digital Enterprise.

Founder and principal analyst at Serious Insights LLC, a boutique IT analysis firm.

Director of Business Insights, Microsoft.
CKO and VP of Knowledge Management at Forrester Research.

Author of Management by Design, Listening to the Future, Rethinking Smart Objects, CyberLife!, Understanding Artificial Intelligence, and Sketches of Spain and other Poems.

Daniel's analysis has appeared in HBR, Strategy+Business, NASA ASK, FastCompany, HR Matters, Wired, Knowledge Management Review, and many other publications.

Former Visiting Liberal Arts Fellow and current instructor, Bellevue College.

Pedro Martins

Founder and General Manager of Singularity Digital Enterprise.

Founder and General Manager of Urbiwise.com's - artificial real estate market intelligence platform.

Expert at the European Commission in Brussels in e-services, e-health and public policies.

Manager in various business areas for 8 years at Microsoft Portugal.

Founder of UMIC (Agência para a Sociedade do Conhecimento) with Diogo Vasconcelos and was Vice President of POSI (Programa Operacional Sociedade da Informação).

Director of Adamastor Capital, one of the first national technology-based venture capital companies of the José de Mello Group, and member of the Executive Committee of eHealth, the group's holding company for new healthcare technologies.

Manager in the Investment Banking area at BCP Bank and MelloValores, at the first Portuguese Online Brokerage Bank - melloinvest.com.

Hugo Cartaxeiro

Founder and Managing Partner of Singularity Digital Enterprise.

Founder and Managing Partner of Urbiwise.com's - artificial real estate market intelligence platform.

Board member of APDC over two consecutive terms.
Sales and Service Manager for 14 years at Microsoft Portugal.

Other professional assignments include business consultancy, IT Services, telecom operators and R&D centers.

Singularity Digital Enterprise

The company was founded in 2016, to transform organizations' data into real competitive advantages for the business, with products and services developed through Data Science, A.I. and Machine Learning. In 2019, Singularity DE created its Power BI & AI Competence Center to develop specialized projects based on the Microsoft Power Platform.

Currently, Singularity DE has a team of 60 people based in Lisbon with a robust client portfolio, which includes the largest Portuguese accounts namely EDP, Microsoft, Galp, AtivoBank, among others. We extract business value from your data through complex algorithms and AI, presenting it with beautiful visualizations.

www.singularityde.com   info@singularityde.com

www.ingramcontent.com/pod-product-compliance
Lightning Source LLC
Chambersburg PA
CBHW030955240526
45463CB00016B/2639